GOD DIDN'T SILENCE ME

GOD DIDN'T SILENCE ME
HE MADE ME HIS MIRACLE

An inspirational message for cancer survivors and their families

BOBBY FLETCHER GARRETT

iUniverse, Inc.
Bloomington

God Didn't Silence Me
He Made Me His Miracle

iUniverse books may be ordered through booksellers or by contacting:

iUniverse
1663 Liberty Drive
Bloomington, IN 47403
www.iuniverse.com
1-800-Authors (1-800-288-4677)

Because of the dynamic nature of the Internet, any web addresses or links contained in this book may have changed since publication and may no longer be valid. The views expressed in this work are solely those of the author and do not necessarily reflect the views of the publisher, and the publisher hereby disclaims any responsibility for them.

Any people depicted in stock imagery provided by Thinkstock are models, and such images are being used for illustrative purposes only.
Certain stock imagery © Thinkstock.

ISBN: 978-1-4759-7987-9 (sc)
ISBN: 978-1-4759-7988-6 (ebk)

Printed in the United States of America

iUniverse rev. date: 03/13/2013

Contents

"Surely goodness and mercy shall follow me all the days of my life, and I shall dwell in the house of the Lord forever."

Psalm 23:6 (KJV)

Miracles: "I Speak it to the Atmosphere"

Miracles are what our eyes see as the impossible but those things that are God's opportunities. They are the opportunity for us to realize the greatness, power, mercy and love of a living God.

Miracles are an act of God. Miracles cannot be summoned, except by God Almighty. Miracles are God's choice of who, what and when He will apply his wonders in our midst.

The four gospel writers recorded 35 miracles performed by Jesus with eyewitness testimony. Approximately twenty three of the 35 miracles dealt with physical healing. Today, miracles are among us daily and we are eyewitnesses to God's power. Do you know someone who has been given a second chance at life? Do you know an addict who has been delivered from demonic drugs? Do you know of survivors of dreadful and frightening diseases? Do you know what God has done for you, a loved one or a friend that could have only been an Act of God?

This little book is about one of God's miracles. With careful attention He has guided my pen as I tell you my story. —*Bobby*

DEDICATION

To my children, Bobbinetta, Barbara, Fred, Nicole, Jay, Eric and Chaunte` who hold the strings to my heart, and to my eleven grandchildren and one great grandchild.

To my wife Alice, my sisters, my brothers and all my nieces, nephews and other relatives, whose love for me and my love for them never left our hearts.

To Reverend Robinson, the officers and members of Saint Matthew AME and my sisters-in-law and brothers-in-law, a heartfelt thank you for your love and prayers.

ACKNOWLEDGEMENT

To God be the Glory! Bob and I are thankful for so many people who through their love, prayers and concerns have made our marriage and our life journey heaven felt. We are thankful to:

Reverend M.B. Robinson and the Saint Matthew AME Church family.

Our families, Garretts and McCulloughs who were always there for us.

Dr. Ornan, Rex Hospital and Dr. Wise, UNC Chapel Hill Hospital for their honesty, care and belief in the work God has trained them to do.

Dr. Hall, an extraordinary man with the heart of an angel.

The Praying Sisters Prayer Group who prayed daily at 6:00 a.m. for us and others.

To Bobbinetta, Fred, Jay, Barbara, Nicole and Eric for bearing through some difficult times.

And finally, to Chaunte` who has been her father's private nurse, traveling partner, confidant and daughter-friend.

To God be the Glory for family, friends, prayer partners, love, and life!

Good Ole Boy

Bob's sister Frances always laughed when she told the story of Bob's wish for himself in life. Once when he was being teased by his older brothers, he told his mother. She encouraged him not to get upset because he was going to be her preacher. Bob replied, "I don't want to be a preacher. I just want to be a *good ole boy*." He was a good man.

INTRODUCTION

I am a believer and a five-time cancer survivor. I am one of God's miracles. God's word is true. Miracles do happen and God allows miracles to be present in our midst each and every day. Those of who know me and have seen me know that I am one of God's living miracles. God chose me to be one of His miracles and through the suffering and pain, I accepted His will for me.

Patience and endurance have always been virtues that I learned from my mother, whose role as my family's matriarch taught me many lessons about God, family, love and living.

Twenty-five years, two decades and a half is a long time for one to live, unknowingly living with a potentially and often deadly disease.

According to my doctors, the cancer, the size of the tip of a ballpoint pen, had been dormant in my larynx for twenty-five years. I lived, laughed, traveled, cried, re-married, fathered my youngest daughter, saw my children married and witnessed the birth of my grandchildren; all the while God was performing His miracle in my life. I was a walking miracle, unknown to me or any person on earth. God's ways are not our ways and His wonders we will never understand. It was twenty-five years to the pronouncement of the cancer in my throat (larynx) since I had given up smoking and drinking. I thank God I did. Since November 1997, I have undergone 35 weeks of radiation treatment, two major operations, each one removing one of my two vocal cords, radiation given in 2006 for prostate cancer and as I write this I am scheduled for chemotherapy once every three weeks. Since the beginning of this book I have undergone another 35 rounds of radiation. I am now a neck breather. I breathe through a trac that replaced the regular route of my swallowing. I no longer have the full use of one of my senses. I no longer use my nose for smelling or breathing and only have limited taste. "Isn't God good? I am His Miracle! I'm still here! I am compelled to share the goodness of the Lord."

NOTE: *Bobby transitioned to be with God on December 1, 2008 at 6:06 AM. I am sharing what he had started before he left and leaving much of what he had to say as he said it. Living a full and productive life until the very end he felt compelled to share his story as an inspiration to others and their families. —Alice*

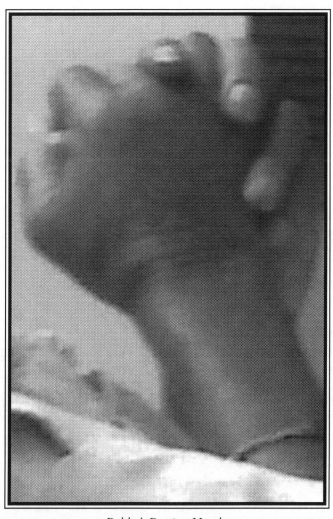

Bobby's Praying Hands
November 29, 2008, 1:31AM
Chaunte' asked her daddy, *"Daddy are you praying?"*
He replied, *"I don't stop."*
The hands of Bobby F. Garrett, an eleven year esophageal cancer
survivor. Taken before his transition on December 1, 2008.

"THE KNOWLEDGE"

I am alive today because my mother taught me to believe in God and how to pray. It was 25 years to the date since I had stopped smoking and taking the little drink that I heard the most life shattering words of all my 63 years.

Being asked to introduce my son as he made the Men's Day speech at my wife's home church was a pleasure. I took it very serious. I meticulously put my introduction together. I knew the scripture reference I would make, I made certain my best suit was pressed and my white shirt ironed to a crisp. I felt that I looked good and was prepared to do a Yeoman's introduction. The proud father I was; I looked the role and was prepared for the task.

After greeting the audience and making my salutation to a church full of friends and kinfolk, I began the introduction of my son. After the first two sentences, I realized discomfort in my throat. I stopped and coughed and set my mind to continue. To my surprise not even a whisper would come forth. I tried! I tried hard to finish the introduction. However, no voice came forth. Finally, just before giving up, my voice came back in a low whisper and I finished with my mouth pressed to the microphone. I was embarrassed to the point of being wet with large beads of sweat. I was embarrassed and frightened. The look on the faces of the church congregation confirmed my fear. I thought I saw fear and disbelief on the faces of my family and friends.

I had not mentioned to anyone the strange, scratchy feeling I had experienced in my throat the past couple of weeks. With throat lozenges and something warm to drink, I had been good to go. I was not heeding the warning God was giving me. As we drove home my wife and I talked about my experience in church. I shared my embarrassment and the fear I felt. After talking about it for a while, I decided to mention the scratchy and strange feeling I had been having in my throat. Neither of us could imagine what it was and decided it might be a cold or some sort of allergy. However, the occurrences of the scratchiness and hoarseness became more frequent.

Doing the Things He Liked To Do

Bob, With Two of His "Girls"

"The Diagnosis"

The scratching in my throat and the sometimes whisper of my voice propelled me to make a doctor visit. After all kinds of tests and my insistence that something was wrong in my throat area, I received the diagnosis. My doctor confirmed after the results of a biopsy that I had throat cancer. I was reluctant about calling Alice, my wife, at work to share the diagnosis. At that time her father had terminal cancer and we had moved him into our home to take care of him. I didn't want to put any more stress on her as her father was terminally ill with prostate cancer and her best friend was also terminally ill with cervical cancer. However, I knew I could not keep it from her. I made the call. She took it better than I expected. We had been praying and fasting for a different report. Taking a biopsy is always a yes or no chance. Yes you have cancer, or no you don't. She quietly said, "God is able and we know who's in charge, we will talk about this when I get home." I was relieved that she was not teary or upset. Without thinking anymore of my results I began to work in the garage, cleaning and throwing out unused items.

We didn't sleep much that night. We lay in the bed holding hands. Our conversation about my diagnosis that night was sprinkled with resignation and determination to find out all we could about the cancer and to seek the best treatment possible. All the while we continued to attend to and take care of my father-in-law. I must add that we were in constant prayer. My youngest brother Carroll was also in the last stage of colon cancer and I was committed to visiting and spending time with him as much as possible.

Our own faith and prayer life was enhanced: by the prayers, concerns, and support of our families, our church family and Reverend Robinson.

> "God never takes us anyplace without equipping us with people, things and events to continue our walk with Him."

Bob at His Best

Family Reunion, Pittsburg, PA

"My Propeller"

I enjoy Sunday School. It is a carry through from my years as a youngster growing up in Laurens, SC. My mother, a strong matriarch insisted that all 10 of my siblings and I not only attend Sunday school but that we be active participants, learning and practicing every role in our local church Sunday School. It was important for us to be active participants. Bethel Hall Church that we attended was the church of both my grandfather and great grandfather. The church today stands on land that was given by one of my ancestors for a church to be built on it. It was fitting and proper that God would use the Sunday School forum to restore my confidence in standing before people with no care that the area of my physical body or my abilities were no longer whole in the eyes of the average person. To me the ability to speak at all represented His goodness and mercy. God favored me by allowing me to continue in my Christian walk. Through my new found skills of using esophageal speech He gave me a forum to learn to participate in Sunday School again. Even more so, God knew I would need the confidence gained as a child to help me to stand as His miracle as a man.

"My Co Pilot on a Long Journey"

"God never takes us anyplace without equipping us with people, things, and events to continue our walk with him."

The trip to the oncologist in November 1997 was a God sent. First of all, the doctor's wife and my wife had worked together as child advocates. He was a friendly man and spared no words in telling me of the rarity of the type of cancer and its seriousness. He referred me immediately to a doctor who specialized in throat cancer. Our visit was immediate. The oncology surgeon examined me and sat with my wife and me to discuss our next steps. We were told that to date November 1997, there were only 500 known cases of that type cancer in the United States. There were only a small number of doctors who could operate on me and surgery was a must. He also shared that any cancer above the shoulder was the fastest growing and if I did not have surgery, I would not live six months. He told us of a friend he had at the University of North Carolina who did larengectomies, the operation for throat cancer. Since it was November and near the holiday season, we asked if we could wait for the surgery. Empathetically, he told us no we needed to get surgery done as soon as possible if Dr. Wise could do it. God being the God He is, when he called for us Dr. Wise was available and agreed to see me.

Bob's Mother

Bob's Dad

Bob, Nora, Mattie and Alice

Bob and His Brothers

Bob with His Brothers Tom and Harold

"My Mother: A Source of Strength"

I could never do my story justice without talking about my mother and her prayers. My mother a practicing Christian taught me and my four brothers and six sisters to live for God and pray. Knowing and doing is something different. I didn't always practice the teachings of my mother but when I did, it was at the right time.

There is no wrong or right time to serve God. He lets us know when we are ready to take our teachings and learning serious and to live out the true meaning of repentance and salvation. Today, I am so glad I found God before my illness. My mother taught me to pray. Daily morning and bed time prayers were a special part of our family routine. My ten siblings and I looked forward to the time when we had to stop our antics and "spend some time with God." Literally we at the time did not look forward to praying but we knew that the time we spent with God gave us a closeness to each other and a time to rest from whatever we were doing . . . wrestling, playing, running, tending to our animals, planting or just sitting around. Early morning prayers were required the minute our feet touched the floor. Mama was a tender hearted lady who orchestrated our praying like she orchestrated our lives. Worship and prayer were the main ingredients. Little did I know that it would be my mother's guidance in developing a prayer life that would sustain me during difficult times. I thank you Mama.

Thank you Mattie.

Bob's Family

Bob, Tom and Uncle Ben

Our Children

Bob with Chaunte'

Bob and His Children

The Grandchildren

God's Goodness and Mercy

"The Removal of the Second Vocal Chord"

Initially I was self conscious of the stoma in my neck. The device, the hole or the tube is vital for me to live. It is my mechanism for breathing. I cough through the device . . . sometimes uncontrollably and not on my own. I no longer have a sense of smell. Really, from my neck up, other than my eyes and ears, I no longer use any of my senses. Seems odd doesn't it? The senses we sometime take for granted becomes a non vital part of me in one way and though non-useful, a vital part of me in another.

Each time I look at my neck areas I am thankful to God that He in His infinite wisdom, gave man the knowledge to repair that part of me, my vocal cords that had been broken through the cancer.

God is a great God. He puts into us so much love, so much time and gives us so much knowledge. He has made His doctors special people who are able to train, retain information, use their hands and their heads to repair His children who are broken, when he deems them to be restored. I think God chose me for restoration.

Only a small percentage of people come down with cancer of the larynx or the common name throat cancer. After the diagnosis of cancer of the larynx, depending upon the needs of the patient and expertise of doctor's, surgery or removal of the larynx or vocal chords is often prescribed. I was blessed to be one of 500 throat cancer patients who initially were fortunate to have a partial largynjectomy. I realized God was giving me a second chance at life.

Earning a Living

Bob and His Prize

Bob and Eric

SLIGHTEST IDEA

Bobby would never allow himself to get embroiled in anyone's affairs, likes or dislikes. When asked his opinion he would reply, "I don't have the slightest idea" and continue doing whatever he was doing. He was everybody's friend and no one's foe.

"The Comeback after a Setback"

The third Sunday in August 2007, I stood before the Sunday School participants at my church and assumed my role as Assistant Superintendent. Many of my fellow parishioners were amazed, even though they had heard me speak many times before, when I carefully put my thumb over the hole in my throat and proceeded to lead them in the devotional. I didn't cough or stumble over my words. God had brought me through my self-consciousness and reluctance to talk or not use the device to cover the hole in my throat. The awkwardness of using my thumb to cover the hole never appeared to me as I went about doing my Father's business. I was grateful to God and to my pastor for allowing me to share my story with my church family.

"Sharing My Story"

My Lay Organization Speech
Saint Matthew AME
October 8, 2006

*"Faith is the substance of things hoped for
and the evidence of things unseen."*

Protocol having been established . . . Good Morning!

Thank you for the wonderful introduction and thank you my church family for accepting me as a Lay Sunday speaker. I am not a speaker but I will do my best to share with you this morning.

*"Faith is the substance of things hoped for
and the evidence of things unseen."*

My topic this morning is: I AM A LIVING WITNESS!

I am a witness for the Lord every day of my life.

I am one of His Miracles.

How many of you have your vocal chords that allow you to talk? I don't have any and yet God allows me to speak and try to sing and communicate with you, my church family, and to share His word when I can.

Let me tell you why I am a living witness and one of God's miracles.

Two times in my life I could have turned myself away from God, because of the blow I was dealt . . . and God could have turned Himself away from me.

- *One time I was out there in the world and the second time I was in the world but in the palm of God's hand and in His word. Both times, God knew who I was and the plans He had for my life.*
- *In 1971 I was sitting in a car in Brooklyn, New York with my back turned to the door when a truck hit the side of the car where I was sitting. I knew I was hurt but I had no idea as to the impact of the collision or the extent of my injury. I lay in the hospital unable to move from my waist down for four months and I was in traction at home for over a year. At 37 years old I was paralyzed from my waist down. A little time after that I became a single parent raising a daughter. I was far from home, not living very close to any relatives except my brothers and sisters in New York. I was living in Linden, New Jersey. After a great deal of therapy and all kinds of tests, the doctor wanted to operate and I refused. One day the doctor came in to release me. I will never forget what he said to me. He told me, "Mr. Garrett, you can go home and be a vegetable," so they installed traction on my bed at my house. I was devastated and I can't tell you that I was the person then in my religion that I am today. I can't tell you that my prayer life was as it is today. But I can tell you that I had a praying mother and I know she prayed for me when I couldn't pray for myself.*

Through her prayers and encouragement I found enough faith to believe that I would walk again. In my bed and in my room I did every exercise that I learned in therapy as much as I could every day of my life. My years at home and at the church and Sunday School led me to have faith that I would walk again. I had learned to walk before I had feeling in my legs. I remember gaining the feeling back in my legs and that gave me the encouragement to continue a very difficult routine.

- *I am walking! I have the use of my limbs. I went back to work. At work, I changed jobs from special duty to carrying mail. Each day I walked I got stronger.*
- *In 1977, God did another miracle for me. He allowed me to meet my lovely and beautiful wife Alice.*
- *Twenty four months later He gave us the gift of our daughter, Chaunte'.*
- *The second blow to shake me was in 1997 when I lost my voice introducing my son at a church. I was embarrassed and sought medical advice to find out why I could not speak above a whisper.*
- *When I met my wife, there were several things I gave up . . . mainly because they were not a part of her life. One of the things I gave up was drinking.*
- *Almost to the date, 25 years after I stopped drinking. I was diagnosed with throat cancer or cancer of the larynx. I was devastated but I was also happy.*
- *I was devastated because I learned it was a fast growing cancer but I was happy that God had allowed it to just lie there dormant for 25 years and not grow at all. It was only the size of a ballpoint pen tip.*

- *The cancer diagnosis, like the paralysis, began a powerful, faithful, and loving walk with God! I am a witness to his grace, mercy and love.*

- *I underwent 12 weeks of radiation on my neck area. I was told I might want to buy some turtleneck shirts because the radiation would burn my neck and might even blister it. We brought the shirts but I never had to wear them. The radiation left no signs or scars. I made it through the radiation without pain and was certain the cancer was gone. I was faithful in my prayers, thanksgiving to God and my regular visits to the doctor.*

- *In April of 2001 during a routine visit to the doctor, I was told the cancer was back and that I would have to be operated on. It was an operation that had been performed only 500 times in the United States. Very few doctors did this kind of operation and they were in great demand.*

- *My doctor just happened to be a friend to a doctor who, if he had time could do the operation for me. I was told that my chance of surviving the cancer with the operation was 50/50 and without the operation, I would not live six months.*

- *We were told that the operation had to be done right away. Within a week, I was operated on by my doctor's friend. Prior to the surgery, I was told I may not be able to talk again without a voice box and they would leave a hole in my neck for a Trek tube. The surgery was to take eight hours but to our surprise it only lasted 4.5 hours.*

- *I only remember that Reverend Robinson, my immediate family and my brother Tom being there with me.*

- *A hole was left in my throat for the tube and I could not eat solid food or speak for a period from May to November. I was fed three times a day through a tube in my stomach. Initially, my family fed me until I gained my strength and learned to feed myself.*
- *I had to learn how to swallow and chew all over again. My relationship with God was all I needed in my silence as I sat and watched the action around me.*
- *I worked on my relationship with God and practiced swallowing and chewing and even sneaked real food when I knew no one was looking.*
- *When I went back to the doctor and they discovered I could talk some . . . they were amazed, even though my voice was weak, I praised God that I had a voice.*
- *The doctors decided to tell me that during the surgery, they had to remove both my vocal chords and voice box. I still have the spot for the hole in my throat, even though it has closed up now.*
- *To man and science, I should not be speaking to you today . . . but with God all things are possible! God is a merciful God and He had mercy on me and I thank Him each and every day.*
- *I thank God that I was a member of this church. I never worried about my wife and family. I knew that God and Saint Matthew would take care of them. I had faith in God and you, my church family here at St. Matthew.*
- *God and Reverend Robinson, my brothers, my family and some members of this church were with me 24 hours a day, reading the Bible, spending the night and relieving my wife. The presence of God and His people strengthened and encouraged me.*
- *During this time, I had time to think.*

- *I had time to know that I would be aware of God's miracles.*
- *I don't take life, service or my relationship with God for granted.*
- *I love life and I love living but I love God more.*
- *Even this year when I again was diagnosed with prostate cancer, I knew not to be anxious but to turn it over to God. I have undergone radiation and chemotherapy for the past 8 months. Upon going to the doctor a few weeks ago, I was told that they could not see a sign of cancer anywhere in my body. I praise God and still know that he has used me and my body as one of His miracles to show His awesome power.*
- *Faith is the substance of things hoped for and the evidence of things unseen.*
- *Sometimes God lets us see . . . JUST LOOK AT ME!*
- *I am a living miracle and I know it!*

I am a witness and everywhere I go . . . I am going to show it . . . and tell it. I praise and honor God and I thank you for allowing me to share it.

Lay Day
October 8, 2006

HE'S DONE ENOUGH

In the very latter stage of Bobby's illness, one Sunday he wanted to go to church. Chaunte' and I painfully dressed him. After we had finally got him dressed and tied his shoes, I said, *"I know you are having a hard time with us having to dress you."* Bobby replied, *"I'm alright and if God never does anything else for me, He's done enough."* He enjoyed church tremendously and got a chance to hear Brenda Judge sing his favorite song, *If God Never Does Anything Else For Me, He Has Done Enough.*

"Finishing His Story" —*Alice*

Most of the time, I feel invisible. I was very much aware of my existence but I was not just a wife to Bob; I leaned on him for so many things. Since the beginning of our relationship I was able to relinquish many of my responsibilities as a young divorcee with a six-year old son. I was sole provider for my family, living in Brooklyn, New York, which was not an easy feat for a migrant from the South. After my two sisters and my brother moved back home I was virtually alone without the help and comfort of the extended family I was accustomed to enjoying.

Next to God, family is everything to us and through the eleven-year ordeal of Bob's sickness; we have come to realize just how much strong families are engrained in our existence. We have enjoyed strong and loving families on both sides. Coupled with a generous and serious prayer life, we have built our family on faith and our love of God and His love for us.

There have been many nights that I was unable to sleep. The carnal side of me wanted to fear the unknown with a sick husband or without him here at all. Fear of the unknown would often shake my desire to put Bob's health, my responsibilities and my tomorrow's in God's hands! Praying daily with my prayer partners, maintaining a close relationship with my pastor and sometime struggling to work in the church and maintain was my primary focal points.

Care giving is an awesome responsibility. I could feel that I had been punished by the years that seemingly robbed Bob of his health and me of an unparalleled and beautiful relationship of many, many joys. On the other hand I could feel that God had chosen me to witness firsthand the unfolding of many miracles. I firmly believe in miracles and I believe God gave me a miracle in my husband. Bob not only showed me how to live but he showed us how to die in the hands of the Lord. I never heard him complain once about pain or his sickness. When he knew the end time was near he let his eyes do the talking for him. He looked upon us with care, concern and most of all love.

We have always been a family who loved to take pictures. The last picture taken of Bobby was one of him taken the Saturday morning before he died. It is the picture of his hands folded in prayer. We decided to make a copy of his hands from the picture and make lapel pins to sell for throat cancer research. We as a family felt it was significant that for two weeks Bobby had not been able to speak to us. When he was asked that morning if he was praying he replied in a clear voice: "I Don't Stop." I thank God because I know in his prayers he always prayed for others as well as himself . . . moreover I know he prayed for me.

Bob and Alice

Alice and Bob

PROLOGUE

Bob uses esophageal speech, one of the earliest forms of communication taught to a laryngectome patient after surgery, known as TEP. Without either of his vocal cords, Bob speaks fluently. He sometimes places his thumb over the hole in his throat (he was trained for the placement to be most effective); other times he uses a plastic device he inserts in the trachea area. Since beginning this book, the plastic device is no longer used, by choice. This device covers the hole and can sometimes be worrisome and uncomfortable.

"Esophageal speech is actually one of the earliest forms of communication taught to individuals who have had the larynx removed. There are organizations that offer total support to laryngectomie rehabilitation (i.e. the International Association of Laryngectomies founded in 1952, www.larynxlink.com.)

Trachea-esophageal puncture with prosthesis is a newer form of speech widely used by many laryngectomes. With a TEP a small puncture is made between the esophagus and trachea through the stomach. A prosthetic device is placed in the puncture, which diverts air form the lungs into the throat and through the mouth to produce speech, much like the vocal cords did. Have you ever spent time with a person who by our account was not whole because of a lost limb, a loss of one of the five senses, a broken spirit or one who has been given the death sentence in prison or in the doctor's office. If so, then you know your own feeling of inadequacy to really deal with the individual. But to live with a person who would be considered less than whole and have them minister to you through acceptance of God's will is awesome and uplifting. Miracles in the flesh authenticate a message to us from God.

Bobby Fletcher Garrett
May 3, 1934-December 1, 2008

Bobby Fletcher Garrett was an 11 year Esophageal and Prostate Cancer patient. The product of a praying family, he was a firm believer in God and His goodness. Throughout his battles, Bobby never lost his faith in God and encouraged hope in his family and all of those who cared for him. After the removal of one of his vocal chords, he declared "The rocks will never cry out for me." With the removal of the last of his two vocal chords and the implantation of a trach, he greeted everyday by saying, "This is the day the Lord has made, I will rejoice and be glad in it." When diagnosed with his final reoccurrence of cancer, he smiled and told his family and friends, "If the Lord never does anything else for me, He's done enough!"

During his transition from his earthly home to his heavenly home, when asked if he was praying, Bobby whispered, "I Don't Stop!" Bobby was a man who went out of his way to help people. He showed all those he touched how extraordinary God is. He did so with the humility of an angel.

Las Vegas-The Last Family Vacation

Bob's Favorite Sunday Afternoon Pastime